Before reading this book, the

· a spelling can represent differ
· the spelling <c> can represent tne sounds 'k' (<u>c</u>at)
  and 's' (<u>c</u>elery)

This book introduces:
· the spelling <c> for the sounds 'k' and 's'
· text at 2 and 3 syllable level

Vocabulary:
scowled   – frowned in an angry way
centipede – a small creature like an insect that has a
            long, thin body and many legs
certainly – of course
chomped   - munched

Talk about the story

Pam doesn't like to eat carrots and
celery. How can Pip persuade her
to eat this healthy food?

Reading Practice

Alternative pronunciations for the spelling <c>.
Practise blending these sounds into words.

'k'	's'
camping	city
clap	cycle
candle	centre
cost	circle
combine	princess
call	excited
come	pencil
magic	December

Carrots and Celery

Pip and Pam sat down to eat lunch.

"Today the menu is carrots and celery!"

Pip announced. "I hate carrots and

I hate celery!" Pam scowled.

1

Pip chopped the celery into strips and the carrots into little circles. He placed them carefully on the plate. "Today's menu is – a bunch of flowers!"

Pip placed the carrot circles in a wiggly line. "Today's menu is – a centipede!"

"I am certainly not eating a centipede!" Pam declared.

"I want to eat cereals instead!" Pam decided. "But carrots and celery are healthy too," Pip said. Then he had an idea.

"Shall we play a game?" asked Pip. "The rule is we eat the carrot circles and celery sticks after we play." "Certainly!" Pam grinned.

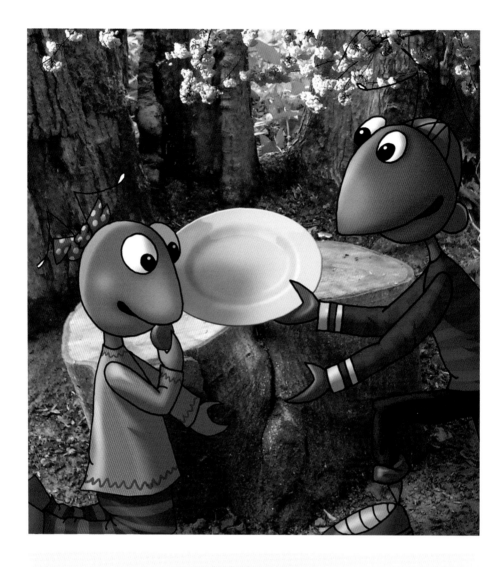

"I win!" Pam declared as she chomped on a carrot. "Let's play again!" They played until there were no carrots or celery sticks left!

Questions for discussion:

- Why does Pam scowl when Pip announces that carrots and celery are on the menu for lunch?

- How does Pip try to persuade Pam to eat the vegetables?

- How does Pip get Pam to eat all the vegetables in the end?

- Why should people eat vegetables?

Reading game with <c> words

Play as pelmanism or use for reading practice. Enlarge and
photocopy the page twice on two different colours of card.
Cut the cards up to play.
Ensure the players sound out the words.

cup	cygnet	across
cell	carrot	cinema
scrub	recent	camera
city	magic	December
picnic	cancel	October